So you really want to l

English
Prep

BOOK 2

Answer Book

So you really want to learn

English
Prep

BOOK 2
Answer Book

Susan Elkin

Series Editor: Nicholas Oulton M.A. (Oxon.)

GALORE PARK

www.galorepark.co.uk

Published by Galore Park Publishing Ltd
19/21 Sayers Lane, Tenterden TN30 6BW
www.galorepark.co.uk

Text copyright © Susan Elkin 2005

Typography by Typematter, Basingstoke
Printed by Biddles

ISBN-10 1 902984 57 9
ISBN-13 978 1 902984 57 5

First published 2005
Re-printed 2006

Accompanying this course:
English Prep Book 1   ISBN 1 902984 53 6
English Prep Book 1 Answer book   ISBN 1 902984 56 0
English Prep Book 2   ISBN 1 902984 66 8

Available in the *So You Really Want to Learn* series:
French
Latin
Spanish
Maths
Science

A word about using this book

So you really want to learn English Prep Book 2 is intended for use both by teachers and parents. This answer book suggests answers to the exercises where appropriate and makes occasional suggestions about how the book might be used, especially by parents for whom the working methods might be unfamiliar.

Some exercises really don't have, or need, answers. In Chapter 9 Exercise 9.6 (page 106), for example, pupils are asked to complete some sentences. They will, of course, come up with a wide range of ideas and none of us can prescribe or predict what these will be. All an assisting adult needs to do is to encourage. Where I think it's appropriate and/or likely to be helpful, I have made suggestions, but these can only be examples of the sort of thing pupils might think of.

Each chapter of the pupil's book begins with three texts for comprehension: one fiction, one non-fiction and a poem. These are themed so that the subject matter shares some common ground across the three items.

Ideally a pupil should read through the text he or she is working on several times and have the opportunity to discuss it with a teacher before attempting the questions. It can help for a teacher to read the text aloud to the pupil first. Or, if he or she can read well enough, the pupil could read it aloud to the adult and/or the rest of the class. Then a second reading might be a silent one – although poetry with its close relationship to music is almost always better heard than read silently.

I've always found that, with a comprehension exercise, it makes sense to work through the questions orally with the pupil first and then set him/her the task of answering them independently in writing. Traditionally, comprehension answers are expressed in complete sentences which repeat part of the question because it reminds pupils of the essential features of a grammatically correct sentence. Mostly, the answers in this book have been slightly abbreviated.

I don't think we can remind ourselves too often that English is not Maths, or even Latin. Of course, there are some questions or items in exercises which have one irrefutable answer. But there are many more which do not – particularly when the question or 'answer' is a response to poetry.

Poets deliberately choose words or phrases for their ambiguity. They want the reader/listener to respond to the word in several different ways at different levels. In the poem *The Zebras* by Roy Campbell on page 119/120 the word 'breathe,' for instance, has connotations of life, moisture, quiet and imperceptible movement – and alert readers will spot and want to comment on more. That's the joy of poetry – but it also means there are few cut and dried answers.

Even in prose writing, often there are different words which mean something similar and many ways of expressing the same idea. That's fine. We want children to be original thinkers. So let's encourage them to think as broadly as possible in their answers and not be too absolute about right and wrong responses. We don't want to limit them.

It means, though, that quite often my suggested answers need to be mentally prefaced with phrases such as 'words to the effect of …' or 'something along the lines of … '. There will usually be other, equally appropriate, and perhaps better, ways of putting it.

And frequently pupils will think of something which I (or you) have not. It happens in the classroom all the time and should be encouraged. My answers are not necessarily definitive. Teachers, and others working with children, have to exercise a bit of humility sometimes. We don't know it all. Far from it.

Each chapter of the pupil's book has a spelling section because, of course, we all want the children in our charge to develop into accurate spellers. Remember, though, that it isn't a particularly useful skill to be able to spell a word aloud letter by letter. For many pupils, in fact, that's quite difficult to do because you have to visualise the word first which is a pretty sophisticated requirement. It is far more important (and generally easier) to learn to write down the words correctly spelled. So when I teach spelling I always get the pupils to write rather than recite.

Teachers of English will have read many of the books I recommend in the 'Have you read ?' sections. So will many parents, but I hope, in this second book, I have made *some* more suggestions which will be new to some adults as well as to children.

If you want to encourage a child to read there is no substitute for reading the same books and enthusiastically discussing that reading with the child. A child who sees respected adults absorbed in reading gets the message that reading is a grown-up, worthwhile activity and something to emulate. The worst thing an adult can tell a child in this context is that he or she is 'too busy to read'. That tells the child that reading is childish. So then, naturally, they see it as part of growing up to read less – or not all.

But if you read books in parallel with 'your' pupil, whether you're a parent or a teacher, it becomes a shared experience, and very special and memorable. This could be yet another way in which parents at home can use *So you really want to learn English Prep Book 2* to develop children's command of English. It's a very 'bookish' book as I tell readers in my introduction (pages 1–2). I make no apology for that.

SJE
July 2005

Contents

Chapter 1

Exercise 1.1

1. (a) good, exciting, traditional, theatrical etc.
    (b) shout, bellow, yell etc.
    (c) prance, leap, rear up etc.
    (d) astride
    (e) for 'lit onto' tickled, touched, struck etc.
    (f) foolish, stupid, silly, taken in etc.

2. The southern United States accent is in the diction: e.g. 'I never see anything so lovely,' 'I couldn't noway understand' and 'everybody just a-howling.' Also the use of dialect words like 'lit' and 'bully' indicate the southern states. (Note these words have a different meaning in Standard English and the difference is worth pointing out to pupils.) The use of superlative forms such as 'splendidest', which in Standard English would be 'most splendid', is also common in this part of the US. In addition, the quaint (to English ears) use of a- prefix: e.g. 'a-reeling' 'a-sailing.

3. Huck was impressed by the circus, riveted by the glittery show business clothes and glamorous (to him) women. He was mesmerised by the movement, sound and slickness of the acts.

4. He feels silly for being fooled by him. He is also sorry for the ringmaster.

5. Huck's character seems to be open (he tells us his inner feelings); imaginative (he is swept along by the theatricality of circus); naïve (he is taken in by a drunk man); inexperienced and young (he is seeing the circus with fresh eyes, presumably for the first time.)

6. Huck's language races along, with one idea after another. It is the language of speech rather than as usually written. (Twain was writing in a completely new way which was very different from earlier nineteenth century novels such as those by Dickens). This style gives a sense of an excited child spilling it all out. In fact, it's very carefully crafted to give this impression.

Exercise 1.2

1. The lions stride in with bottoms swaying. The have big paws – a large version of a domestic cat's feet. They sit on little stools, looking sad with dead eyes, and roar when the keeper / tamer / handler signals.

2. (a) The sunshine on the bars of the cage makes shadow stripes on lions, like zebras. But unlike zebras which are free, these lions are in captivity. Zebra stripes symbolise imprisonment.

    (b) 'Abdicated' is usually used only of kings and queens – lions are traditionally the 'king of the jungle.' Not any more.

3. This introduces rhythm in repetition, while the long vowels suggest gloom.

4. The pupil might choose phrases such as 'provided kill' (lions should be catching their own. 'Kill' is ironic as they haven't killed it); 'bored theatrical roar' (the half rhyme of 'bored' and 'roar' evokes the sound of lions. 'Theatrical' suggests it's pretended).

5. The poet is against performing animals. He suggests free existence in the wild is better.

6. He imagines they are resigned to their fate. They are not even trying to escape.

Exercise 1.3

1. (a) displayed, showed off, walked up and down etc.

    (b) have nothing to do with, avoid etc.

2. They are using 16 animals.

3. She is used as an advertisement. Audiences are encouraged to photograph her during intervals in the show.

4. It is because she didn't really escape. She was quickly recaptured.

5. Anne left the circus when she got the chance in Scotland.

6. There are health problems and too little space. Constant moving from town to town is unsettling, elephants need a herd to live with, they're intelligent and they don't like 'urban' noise such as joy-riders.

7. Bobby Roberts says that the circus people love Anne and take care of her. Anne has been performing for 45 years and would miss it because she knows no other life. (He also argues that the circus is 50 years old and people of Timperley enjoy the circus – both reasons are irrelevant but given as reasons in the narrative. You could point out to pupils that these points are part of the circus people's attempt to deflect attention from the real issues.)

Exercise 1.5

Accept anything reasonable pupils come up with. Here are some examples:

Adjectives: successful, tearful, bashful, purposeful, colourful, shameful, spiteful, fearful, harmful, hateful.
Nouns: fistful, pocketful, bucketful, shovelful, mouthful, jugful, houseful, earful.

Exercise 1.6

1. Louis Pasteur (pasteurisation).

2. Adolphe Sax (saxophone).

3. Monsieur Nicot (nicotine).

4. Lord Sandwich (sandwich).

5. Dr Rudolph Diesel (diesel).

6. Alessandro Volta (volts).

7. Duke of Wellington (wellington boots).

8. Charles Macintosh (macintosh).

9. Louis Braille (braille).

10. Laszlo Biro (biro).

Exercise 1.8

1. <u>Mark Twain</u> was American.

2. <u>Lions, tigers</u> and <u>panthers</u> are big <u>cats</u>.

3. As the <u>Land Rover</u> moved forward with <u>caution</u>, we saw a single <u>elephant</u> and then a whole <u>herd</u>.

4. The <u>circus</u> is coming to <u>town</u>.

5.   <u>Anne</u> waved her <u>trunk</u> and then, to our <u>joy</u>, she trumpeted.

6.   <u>Hunger</u> was gnawing at me so I ate some <u>biscuits</u>.

Exercise 1.9

This is a free-for-all exercise but here are some suggestions. Encourage pupils to range as widely as possible.

1.   advised / told / instructed.

2.   have passed / will come / would have succeeded.

3.   consume / were eating / will attack.

4.   dance … watch / was riding … were walking / could have spoken … would have heard.

5.   ask / shoot / cry.

6.   grabbed … mounted / was watching … wondering / will clean … rest.

Exercise 1.10

Another free-for-all. These are just examples:

1.   Let's <u>part</u> those briars (verb).
     A madrigal is a <u>part</u> song (adjective).
     <u>Part</u> of the trouble is your attitude (noun).

2.   I <u>mean</u> that! (verb).
     A miser is <u>mean</u> (adjective).
     The <u>mean</u> is 25 (noun). N.B. 'mean' is another word for an average.

3.   I can't <u>lift</u> that load (verb).
     The school <u>lift</u> is out of action (noun).
     They were digging a <u>lift</u> shaft (adjective).

4.   Ramadan is a <u>fast</u> for Muslims (noun).
     Cheetahs can run <u>fast</u> (adverb).
     We caught the <u>fast</u> train (adjective).

5.   I pasted a <u>strip</u> of purple paper at the top of my art work (noun).
     Let's <u>strip</u> away the layers (verb).

6.   The <u>flower</u> bed was very attractive (adjective).
     I'm waiting for the bulbs to <u>flower</u> (verb).
     A lily is a colourful <u>flower</u> (noun).

Exercise 1.11

1.   What a book!

2.   One of my favourite authors is Mark Twain.

3.   Have you read all Cecil Day Lewis's poems?

4.   Shall I pour the tea?

5.   No I won't!

6.   It is quite easy to punctuate accurately.

Chapter 2

Exercise 2.1

1. (a) Luxuriantly. Plenty of natural growth and life.
    (b) Came gently to an end without a definite boundary.
    (c) Military stronghold, 'standing like a fort'. Implications of defence and strength but quite kindly – rather old fashioned as in a children's story.
    (d) Experiment with. Also a sense of tasted with enjoyment – the sensation is novel.
    (e) Sweet scented: 'the scent spilled over them', and herbal.
    (f) A dramatic 'pause'.

2. They want to find out where they are and what the island is like.

3. They need to find food.

4. Ralph seems to be emerging as the leader. He makes judgements and has dignity. He says: 'This belongs to us' and 'That's the quickest way back.' He is less impetuous than Jack and he is assertive and charismatic ('cupping gesture'). He speaks 'wisely.'

5. Jack is practical. The narrative uses the terms 'Hunt; Catch things' and 'Steeper'. He is dismissive of Ralph's thoughtfulness about the candles and says: 'We can't eat them. Come on.' He is a boy of action. He knows they should kill the piglet and he comes close to doing it.

6. The island is boat-shaped and is steeper at one end than the other. It is near another island which is a single rock. It is tropical, mountainous, bound by coral reef with turquoise water within it – a lagoon. The island is probably uninhabited and has many flowers and butterflies, aromatic shrubs and wild pigs.

7. The boys feel ashamed because killing a piglet is alien to 'civilised' boys from towns in Britain. They realise how close they've come to a very primitive action which would be forbidden at home. The narrative observes: '…what an enormity the downward stroke would be.'

Exercise 2.2

1. (This is a possible answer – there are many other ways of expressing it.) The Germans shot down an allied aircraft over occupied Crete in 1941 but failed to guard the wreckage properly. To spite and ridicule the Germans, three local youths set fire to it. Because the Germans threatened the whole local population the three gave themselves up. Two were condemned to death by firing squad and the youngest imprisoned. One of the condemned young men took his executioners by surprise and escaped.

2. The poet compares it to a whale which 'sank' and was 'bleeding'; the sky is compared to the surrounding sea and the landing site to the ocean bed. This is an effective sustained metaphor because the size of the aircraft is about right and gives a sense of it as a living thing.

3. (a) He looked at bright sun with half closed eyes – sense of gritty determination.
    (b) A tune which regularly introduces something or someone on TV or radio so that the audience associates the tune with the programme. Here he means a tune to remember him by. This is bitter irony because he's going to die, and is associated with something a lot less trivial than entertainment.
    (c) Infinite, unending, permanent.
    (d) This really means the rhythm of waves but also here suggests the desire for revenge and justice which gnaws at 'his comrade' until eventually he returns as a soldier.

4. The poet is pointing out the absurdity of sentencing the three differently on the grounds of age. Do you have to be a certain age to face a firing squad? Was the younger boy any less responsible? Can this possibly be justice? (If you are discussing this with a class you could mention the 1953 case of Craig and Bentley in which a British policeman was shot in Croydon by an under-age Craig who subsequently went to prison. Bentley hanged because he was over 18 although he hadn't pulled the trigger.)

5. It could be argued either way but it probably ends positively. Some good came out of the incident. The third man eventually returned to his birthplace and was able to help 'like an archangel' to restore what is right.

6. The rhyme scheme adds irony to the poem. It races along like a nursery rhyme but the content is serious. It helps to make fun of the German invaders in phrases such as 'And, grey in the guardhouse, seven Berliners / Lost their stripes as well as their dinners.'

Exercise 2.3

1. The rescues were completed at 7am on Monday 16 August 2004.

2. He was warned by Mr and Mrs Shute. He clung to a tree.

3. There is no evidence – everything in this article could have come from telephone interviews.

4. He was a Master Aircrewman of 203 Squadron at RAF St Mawgan. He is resourceful as he found a way of lifting baby Senara to safety using a rucksack; and the baby's mother says he was '…great, really kind and gentle.'

5. It shows the seriousness of the emergency. They needed reinforcements from all over Britain, particularly from Scotland which is many hundreds of mile away.

6. They focused on the baby because it adds human interest for readers.

Exercise 2.5

Here are some examples – the pupils will think of others.

1. mousehole, mousetrap
2. lacewing, lacemaking
3. noiseless, noisenik
4. biteless, biting
5. requirement, requiring
6. priceless, pricing
7. shoehorn, shoelace
8. freedom, freefall
9. serviceable, serviceman
10. peaceful, peaceable

Exercise 2.6

1. circumvent
2. circumlocution
3. circumference
4. circumfluous
5. circumscription
6. circumspect

Exercise 2.7

1. Manchester
2. Paris
3. London
4. Naples
5. Liverpool
6. Sicily
7. Oxford
8. Hamburg
9. Glasgow
10. Florence

Exercise 2.8

These are just examples. Anything which makes sense of the words is acceptable.

1. Because I cried for a very long time over something she thought was minor, my mum told me not to overreact.
2. School policy is not to overburden pupils with prep.
3. If you're going to a casual party, it's best not to overdress.
4. Most pupils address teachers formally by their title and name, because to do otherwise would be overfamiliar.
5. Overcast skies usually mean rain to come.
6. If you overdraw at the bank you take out, or try to take out, more money than is in your account.
7. There is an overlap between English and almost all other subjects.
8. I know you don't care for eavesdropping, but did you happen to overhear where we're going for tonight's surprise supper?
9. The boys in *Lord of the Flies* were looking for ways to overcome their difficulties.
10. I hope Mr Clarkson will overlook at least some of my spelling mistakes.

Exercise 2.9

1. <u>twining</u> (line); bald (spot)
2. <u>red</u> (face)
3. <u>grey, seven</u> (Berliners)
4. <u>dramatic</u> (rescue)
5. <u>well-respected, admired</u> (Charles Causley); <u>fine</u> (poet)
6. <u>thin, eager</u> (they)

Exercise 2.10

1. sadly
2. extremely
3. still
4. fast
5. dismally, reluctantly
6. forwards, backwards, clockwise

Exercise 2.11

Remember, there are no commas before 'and' or other conjunctions, of course.

1. 'Peter, please bring the paper, glue, stapler and pens.' (A comma after vocative, and to separate the nouns in the list.)
2. 'Did you see that enormous, slinky, black cat?' (Commas to separate the adjectives in list.)
3. 'What an amazing story, Jake!' (A comma to mark off the name of the person addressed; vocative.)
4. We heard Perry playing, singing and tuning his violin while his twin sister Abigail was outside trampolining, catching, throwing and exercising. (Commas to separate the verbs in two separate lists of verbs.)
5. 'Everybody, will you listen, please!' (Commas separate the vocative 'everybody' and the word 'please'.)
6. Maria's Tuesday lessons included Maths, PE, Geography, English and French. (Commas to separate the nouns in the list.)
7. 'Sit down, Melissa, and I'll explain.' (A pair of commas fencing off the vocative from the rest of the sentence, like parenthesis.)

Chapter 3

Exercise 3.1

1. (a) trying it out, seeing it if works, not very confident.
   (b) saying something obvious in a way which pretends to be serious but is really trying to be witty.
   (c) break out, give birth to in a violent way like a volcano producing lava.

2. She is making a public point about equality. She's black and 'superior' but she wants to ignore the differences. Also, she is very attached to / interested in Callum.

3. Sephy tells it in detail because getting food is ordinary. The gesture she makes by sitting with Callum is not ordinary, by contrast. Also the food is not special – it is dull and unappetising. School dinners are the same for everyone, the one thing which really is equal, perhaps.

4. The brown of the sticking plaster on the pink skin is very prominent. Sephy notices and is sympathetic but she had never thought of the problem before. It is a symbol of all the tiny things which make life difficult for the 'wrong' group in an 'alien' culture. The author is making the point that in real life most plasters are 'flesh coloured,' i.e. pink, but many users are black.

5. Both of these descriptions are very vivid. 'Like a throbbing thumb' suggests pain and neatly compares something felt (the throbbing thumb) with something seen (plaster). It shows Sephy identifying with Shania and being sensitive to her situation. 'Like a python on steroids' is humorous and irreverent. It is a typically dismissive attitude of a pupil towards the teacher behind the latter's back. Sephy is bright and original.

6. She realises that Callum doesn't want to be seen with her in public.

7. Callum is upset, guilty and annoyed with himself (and with Sephy for causing the incident). He wishes things were otherwise. He knows he has hurt Sephy and vents his anger in a physical activity.

Exercise 3.2

1. He knows that he'll suffer a 'wasted journey' when she finds out that he is black. He wants to get the issue out of the way. The word 'confess' suggests that he ought to feel remorse for his colour but he doesn't. He is not ashamed. It is a use of irony.

2. She is concerned about his degree of blackness.

3. (a) feigned, put on, forced by the situation to act a role.
   (b) sour, stale, acidic, foul smelling.
   (c) agreement, saying yes.

4. The old-fashioned telephone box. It was still legal for landlords to question applicants about their colour and to refuse the room on race grounds. (It would be helpful to tell pupils that it used to be common for notices in windows in Britain to say: 'Room to Let – No Blacks'. The 1960s' anti-discrimination legislation stopped the use of this type notice.)

5. African, very dark, very light, plain or milk chocolate, West African sepia, brunette, peroxide blonde, raven black.

6. (a) The narrator is highly educated. He knows that she won't be able to detect his nationality / colour from his voice. He uses educated language, e.g. 'spectroscopic' and 'simplification' in his own thoughts. He thinks quickly. When he realises that he is not going to get the room, he jokes 'West African sepia' at her expense.

(b)   The woman doesn't understand his vocabulary or humour but senses that she is being laughed at and feels disadvantaged. 'Truthfulness clanged her accent' – she stops putting on a voice once she is really rattled. She is much less well educated.

7.   He mentions it to insult her and get his own back in a light-hearted way, but only once he knows she won't let him rent her room.

8.   The features include the use of short lines; many phases which are not grammatical sentences e.g. 'Stench / Of rancid breath of public hide-and-speak.' Blank verse with uneven rhythm mirrors the jerkiness of the situation. There is a clear patterning in lines like 'The rest of me. Palm of my hand, soles of my feet'. There is poetic repetition in lines such as 'Red booth. Red Pillar Box, Red double-tiered …'. There are also poetic devices, such as alliteration and consonance, e.g. 'Silence. Silenced transmission of/Pressurised …'

Exercise 3.3

1.   According to Martin Luther King it was Mississippi.

2.   (a)   long practised, older people with much experience, people who have suffered for many years.
     (b)   parts of a city where a single race or religious group lives or is forced to live.
     (c)   beliefs, usually religious.
     (d)   lifted, raised up, celebrated.

3.   There are two key points which emerge from his speech:
     (a)   freedom and equality for every black American.
     (b)   that there are no social barriers between races.

4.   (a)   If you suffer through no fault of your own you will grow through it, be saved and eventually rewarded.
     (b)   All Americans could one day be like brothers - without discord. This would be as beautiful as a harmonious piece of music.

5.   The language of his speech portrays a basic Christian message – the brotherhood of man. He uses biblical language, in examples such as 'The glory of the Lord', 'every valley shall be exalted' and 'all flesh.'

6.   The speech uses very direct language. It is clearly addressed to 'you.' It is a passionate speech with no humour or irony. The repetition, which is tiresome in writing, is effective in speech. The speech is not a reasoned argument – it is an appeal to the emotions.

7.   Repetition is a key element in rhetoric. Repetition is used for emphasis. There is a stress on 'go back' and 'I have a dream'. Each repetition draws the audience in more closely. (You might look at Churchill's World War Two speeches, St Crispin's Day speech from *Henry V* or Mark Antony's funeral oration for Caesar in *Julius Caesar* for comparison.)

Exercise 3.5

laboratories alloys ladies apologies flies entries buoys Mondays kidneys symphonies

Facetious contains all five vowels – a e i o u – in alphabetical order.

Exercise 3.6

1. A range of action.
2. An instrument for looking at objects a long distance away – such as at the stars.
3. A magnifying instrument for studying items (e.g. bacteria) which would be invisible to the naked eye.
4. A cylindrical children's toy containing mirrors and coloured paper. It makes symmetrical patterns when it is shaken.
5. A right-angled instrument with mirrors used in submarines for surveying the horizon above the water level.
6. A medical instrument which is used for listening to the heart and lungs.
7. A range of seven colours as in a rainbow.
8. Ghostly – it relates to an apparition or spectre which has been seen.
9. Something exceptionally interesting to look at.
10. To watch, as at a sports event.

Exercise 3.7

These sentences are just examples.

1. We had to write a discursive essay expressing our views about racial equality.
2. Martin Luther King's condemnation of inequality is very powerful.
3. The sticking plaster incident in *Noughts and Crosses* is illustrative of the inconveniences faced daily by racial minorities.
4. Ghosts are, in my opinion, entirely illusory.
5. It was an opportune moment to get Mrs Hardy to listen to our complaints.
6. The severity of our new teacher's manner worried us.
7. Sophie, who can run a mile in 4 minutes, asked me to include an adjectival clause in this sentence.
8. It is hard to quantify the benefits to English which come from wide reading, but we all know they are there.
9. 'I think it's time to stop,' opined the headmaster.
10. Before we can analyse a sentence we must ascertain which word or words form the main verb.

Exercise 3.8

1. although / but
2. and ... also
3. despite / notwithstanding
4. as / because
5. although / and / but / whereas / after
6. or / though / but

Exercise 3.9

1. who (relative)

2. this ... that (either way round, both demonstrative)

3. this, that (demonstrative)

4. that, this (demonstrative)

5. which, that (relative)

6. whom (relative)

7. whom (relative)

8. these (demonstrative)

Exercise 3.10

As explained in the preamble to this exercise, some of these commas are optional. It is worth discussing with pupils whether they (or you) would, or wouldn't use them, and why. Such discussion 'cements' the learning.

1. If it is fine tomorrow, I should like to play cricket.

2. Although I have read many of Wole Soyinka's poems, I have yet to see any of his plays.

3. When I saw how tired she looked, I decided not to tell her of our plans but she asked me about them, saying how interested she was, so I had no choice.

4. In May this year, Emma Courtenay joined our school as a member of Year 7 and, as she loves maths, she is actively looking for ways of doing more, getting really good marks and taking GCSE early.

5. Meanwhile Mrs Bawden had crept up on Sephy, silent and determined.

6. Shall we pack up now, carry on for a bit longer, take a break or get ourselves a drink of tea, coffee or juice to sip while we're working?

Chapter 4

Exercise 4.1

1. (a) vibrating, shifting, moving between the two.
    (b) in a cloudy, fuzzy or vague way.
    (c) changed, transformed.

2. (a) 'replenish our insides'. (line 23)
    (b) 'appearing to utter enough invectives to consign the whole parish to perdition'. (lines 49, 50)
    (c) 'ran obliquely into the principal thoroughfare'. (lines 25, 26)

3. There are 15 men in the choir, which you know because Hardy writes 'thirty concentrated eyes'.

4. Her hair was loose and untidy for bedtime. It was normally only seen tidy and 'up'.

5. The use of the phrase 'window architrave.' There is an accurate description of a window at Farmer Shinar's house. Also the description of the wide upper windows and broad bay window.

6. He is annoyed and outraged by Farmer Shinar's attribute to a seasonal tradition.

7. Possibly Dick has gone back to the first house in the hopes of another glimpse of the girl with the loose hair; or he got fed up and had gone home; or he has met a friend.

8. We might have guessed this from the use of the phrase: 'up stroke previously to pouring forth the opening chord'. He knows the price of a 'fiddle' and that it shouldn't be left outside in the damp and why.

Exercise 4.2

1. Preparations described include: decorating churches with yew and holly, paper chains etc. inside homes; flags in the streets; festive shop windows; present giving.

2. (a) It means the coming. It is a church season which is four Sundays before Christmas and anticipates the birth of Jesus.
    (b) Belonging to the local authority or council, collectively owned.
    (c) Cheap, crowded flats.

3. The vocabulary used is no longer in common use, e.g. 'public-houses', 'slacks' (for women's trousers), 'tenements', 'tramcars'.

4. If there is truth in the Christian message that 'God was man' then the bells and presents of a conventional British Christmas are absurdly trivial in comparison.

5. It gives a sense of movement and growth as the poem moves towards the climax of its last verse, like a slow crescendo in music. It adds affectionate wit, e.g. 'Bath salts and inexpensive scent / And hideous tie so kindly meant.'

6. (a) The phrase 'pigeon -haunted classic towers' is a clear rhythmic four beat line with four words stressed, like a drum beat. Towers are an everyday sight of London. Pigeons are like grey ghosts occupying the towers and making their presence felt. The phrase is very atmospheric, conjuring up London on a winter afternoon.
    (b) 'Hideous' is a strong word and it creates nice contrast with the mild, polite word 'kindly.' The phrase is effective because it sums up the reality of present giving for many people, with the present receivers often disliking what they are given.

Exercise 4.3

1. (a) actually, physically etc.
    (b) non-believer etc.
    (c) tolerance, patience, restraint etc.
    (d) strength, resistance etc.

2. He is believed to have put on the first nativity play.

3. The writer believes it teaches children about their culture; it is a long tradition that teaches children important truths about life and human spirit.

4. Some teachers who don't believe in God won't do the Nativity play; certain schools don't want to do it as they worry it might offend children of other religious groups.

5. It establishes her as an ordinary 'mum'. This draws the reader in because it gives them something in common with the writer. It provides human interest on which newspapers, especially those like the *Daily Mail*, thrive.

6. She means that Christianity is 2000 years old and as it began to spread into Europe very early it has influenced law, attitudes, art, literature, church buildings and music etc. in most of Europe for centuries. (Examples include: the Magna Carta, whose laws were not based on retribution, 'an eye for an eye,' like some of Islamic and Jewish law; the Messiah by Handel; Leonardo Da Vinci's The Last Supper; Durham Cathedral; Notre Dame in Paris etc.)

7. Unlike Thomas Hardy's, Susan Elkin's style involves short sentences, short paragraphs, no dialogue, no dialect, more non-Latinate vocabulary, more statement sentences. She also uses some informal language, e.g. 'weepy mums and grans' and 'Don't let's.'

Exercise 4.5

1. fries, enjoys

2. purifies

3. strays

4. supplies, tries

5. amplifies

6. denies, buys, says

Exercise 4.7

theology – study of the nature of God
chronology – study of history to establish dates
archaeology – study of ancient history through excavation
neurology – study of the human nervous system
ornithology – study of birds
musicology – study of music as an academic subject
zoology – study of animals
anthropology – study of human beings
astrology – study of the stars
meteorology – study of the weather

Exercise 4.8

These are just examples. Pupils will think of others.

1. strolled, ambled, strode.
2. encapsulates, depicts, shows.
3. cheerful, happy, lively.
4. fast, rapidly, fluently.
5. politeness, civility, thoughtfulness.
6. laugh, snigger, chuckle.

Exercise 4.9

Make sure that the words in the pupil's answer are all used as prepositions rather than another word class. They should link two nouns or pronouns in terms of where they are. For example:

1. This work is beyond me.
2. Peter sat beside John. (not 'besides' which is an adverb)
3. We shall go away during the summer holiday.
4. Put a question mark after a question.
5. That will put the cat among the pigeons.
6. Don't go without me.
7. The sheets are in the drawer under the bed.
8. The dog ran past the pillar-box.
9. My granny lives by the seaside.
10. My mother drove smoothly into the tunnel.

Exercise 4.10

Here are 50 words to start you off. The pupils will find many more.

acid, acted, antic, café, cart, clear, created, crane, crate, dale, dare, date, defeat, define, drain, earl, eaten, enact, enter, face, fade, fare, fear, frail, frantic, idea, inert, infer, inter, lace, laid, lair, learn, life, liner, nail, neat, need, race, rate, raid, rain, rife, rifle, tail, tear, trace, treat, trade, trail.

Exercise 4.11

'It looks nice warm exercise that, doesn't it?' he enquired of Wardle.
'Ah! It does indeed,' replied Wardle. 'Do you slide?'
'I used to do so on the gutters when I was a boy,' replied Mr Pickwick.
'Try it now,' said Wardle.
'Oh do, please Mr Pickwick!' cried all the ladies.
'I should be happy to afford you some amusement,' replied Mr Pickwick, 'but I haven't done such a thing these thirty years.'

Chapter 5

Exercise 5.1

1. (a) almost unnoticeable, very slight.
   (b) restrained, sad, uncommitted.
   (c) outlive, live / last longer than.

2. Aaron's family name is Winthrop.

3. (a) Aaron is in love with Eppie and has known her a long time. He wants to marry her but plans for Silas to live with them. He knows Eppie won't abandon her father. He is very courteous and thoughtful in his dealings with Silas.
   (b) Mrs Winthrop is wise and is respected by Silas. She has brought Aaron up well. She is Eppie's godmother.

4. Silas looks to the future knowing he will get old. He wants Eppie to be happy and to be looked after, but he is slightly sad that's she's growing up so that things have to change. He is fond of Aaron and trusts him.

5. She wants to talk to her father first and she doesn't want to upset him. She is really quite happy as things are but is beginning to realise she must make a decision.

6. The following are examples only:
   (a) 'Please let's go to see that show, Daddy,' Clare pleaded ingenuously. 'Tickets are only sixty pounds each.'
   (b) 'How many times have I told you that twelve twelves are a hundred and forty four?' demanded the maths teacher emphatically.
   (c) Told in assembly about the appalling accident, we filed meditatively out of the hall.

Exercise 5.2

1. To a 'lovely' and 'fair' woman whose beauty is like 'eternal summer.' To a woman he loves.

2. She reminds him of a fine day in May. But when summer moves on its beauty fades, whereas her attractiveness will last forever because he has described her in a poem. 'So long lives this [the poem] and this gives life to thee.' (He was right in a sense for we continue to enjoy this unknown woman's beauty over 400 years later because we read about her in this sonnet.)

3. (a) the sun.
   (b) her beauty which will never die.

4. Lease is a legal term meaning the length of time you can occupy premises. So in this context it means summer can only stay for a fixed time (and it isn't long) because it will soon be overtaken by autumn and then winter. Summer is personified by being compared with a short-stay tenant.

5. The rhyming links meaning and ideas. 'Shines' and 'declines' are opposites, while 'fade' and 'shade' both suggest dying down. When you hear a rhyme in a sonnet like this you unconsciously listen for the next. You then compare one with the other as they pass.

6. It means that the words of the sonnet will last as long as the human race. As long as there are people (breathing and looking at things) to read it, the woman it is addressed to (his beloved) will still be beautiful. (This splendid piece of hyperbole is fairly typical of Shakespeare and other Elizabethan sonneteers. It is worth pointing out to pupils that the end couplet is entirely monosyllabic which makes it very firm and final.)

Exercise 5.3

1. Valentine had been dead for 78 years.
2. (a) guesswork, speculation etc.
   (b) assigned etc.
   (c) artwork, illustrations, interpretations etc.
3. Geoffrey Chaucer wrote *The Canterbury Tales* in the 14th century.
4. Turni is in Italy, 60 miles from Rome.
5. 14th February has been regarded as the traditional day for birds to start mating for at least seven centuries. So it seemed appropriate for humans also to choose lovers on this day.
6. St Valentine seems a rather light-weight saint because of his association with lovers and not much is known about him. Churches may prefer their patron saint to be someone whose life they can celebrate (and possibly copy) in a more informed way. It is also difficult that there are two St Valentines making it hard to know which one they're dedicated to!

Exercise 5.5

The field is wide open here. They should think of lots of words such as:

tidy – tidiness
silly – silliness
unhappy – unhappiness
sleepy – sleepiness
early – earliness
messy – messiness

Exercise 5.6

These are examples only:

1. She told us that her parents had won the lottery, but it was a falsehood.
2. I wish work didn't take my father abroad so much, but that is his livelihood.
3. Martin Luther King argued for the brotherhood of man.
4. There isn't much likelihood of our getting a family holiday this year because my parents have already used up all their leave.
5. I have an aunt, now the Revd Mary Johnson, who was one of the first British women to enter the priesthood.
6. There is very little crime in our neighbourhood because everyone in the community works hard to prevent it.

Exercise 5.7

This is open-ended. But don't forget the exercise calls for verbs so don't let nouns and adjectives such as 'overcoat' and 'underhand' creep in.

Possibilities include:

overtake, overturn, overrule, overwork, oversee, undertake, undercook, underestimate, undervalue, undermine

Exercise 5.8

There is plenty of scope here. Be aware of these possible meanings:

sit down (at a meal).
ask out (invite).
take in (absorb, understand).
sit up (apply yourself).
ask around (make enquiries).
take out (a portable meal, especially in an American-style fast food establishment. Escort, in the 'dating' sense).
sit back (relax, stop making an effort).
ask in (invite).
take up (adopt, accept).
sit out (decline, in the sense of not taking part in a game, dance etc.).
sit at (a meal or a meeting).

A good dictionary will provide a wide range of meanings for phrasal verbs.

Exercise 5.9

1. brake
2. stop
3. apply
4. left (the meeting; omit 'of')
5. omit
6. substitute

Exercise 5.10

1. They've reached home earlier than we'd expected.
2. Fred's cat and Maura's dog seemed to be making friends.
3. I've just finished reading George Eliot's *Adam Bede* and shall now begin Wilkie Collins's *The Woman in White*.
4. My three school dresses are all too small so we were going to put them away in my younger sister's wardrobe.
5. *Lovers' Vows* is the name of an old play which features in Jane Austen's *Mansfield Park*.
6. Boys' names and girls' names are listed in the back of my granny's dictionary.

Chapter 6

Exercise 6.1

1. (a) passed slowly with a sense of wandering and time not moving in a straight line.
   (b) soothingly, like a lullaby or something which lulls her to sleep.
   (c) disappeared, melted away, evaporated, broke up, dissolved.

2. (a) 'glowing oriflames of fire'
   (b) 'dull pulsating roar'

3. (a) The wombat is not a meat eater so the children are no good as food.
   (b) The tiger cat is carnivorous but, as prey, the children are too big.

4. She feels responsible because she is older and has always looked after him like a mother.

5. It was a cargo plane whose port engine caught fire so that flames got inside the plane. The plane then crashed to the ground and the children had run to safety just before the plane exploded, killing the crew.

6. It is the forgetting and blanking out of memories which are too terrible to live with.

Exercise 6.2

1. (a) impudent
   (b) raconteur
   (c) stark
   (d) romance

2. Christabel Burniston was 94 when the new edition of her book was published.

3. She means a joyful exploration of traditional rhyming and rhythmic poetry for fun without having to follow a syllabus which might insist that modern intellectual poetry in blank verse is studied.

4. She liked the fact he was charismatic and knew a lot of poetry by heart, which he was very skilled at speaking entertainingly. She thought he had a lot of charm but was 'safely' married.

5. The author wanted to wear makeup and, as she saw it, look pretty and feminine. Her mother thought that cleanliness and plain living mattered more.

6. That they were beautiful, perfect, and idealised. They had pale skins and wore medieval clothes (girdles) to model in.

Exercise 6.3

1. His clothes are worn out and too small. He has a dirty neck, untidy hair and his feet are bleeding, suggesting he wears no shoes.

2. He lives with his father and grandmother, both of whom are heavy drinkers. His father drinks beer, his grandmother gin and they both drug Timothy with aspirin to keep him quiet. His mother has abandoned the family and gone off with a soldier.

3. The Winters family may not be breaking the (1950s) law, and there are laws against taking children away from their families. It is very hard for a social worker to act because the law puts difficulties / safeguards in their way.

4. 'Amen' means 'so be it'. Perhaps angels, meaning someone or something kindly and merciful, could arrive and do something for Timothy. Amen means we all agree.

5. It gives the poem momentum, making it roll along unstoppably like Timothy's rotten childhood. It also makes it memorable and easy to learn.

6. (a) Education washes over Timothy because things like arithmetic, which are free and bird-like in the minds of more fortunate children, don't seem relevant among his much greater struggle to simply survive. He ignores lessons or even disrupts ('shoots down dead') them.

   (b) He puts it like this because it is a colourful idea and creates a strong visual image.

Exercise 6.5

These are examples only:

1. Thanks are due to all, though Mr Jones has done the most.
   Although I dislike peas I ate everything on my plate.

2. Let us look at all ways before we make a decision.
   I always check my answers carefully.

3. They all, most of them in uniform, cheered.
   He had almost finished speaking.

4. The family went all together to church.
   If you wear red trousers with a red shirt and red shoes, it is altogether too much.

Exercise 6.6

1. Ceres, goddess of nature

2. Mercury, messenger of the gods

3. Jove, chief god associated with good humour

4. Venus, goddess of love

5. Vulcan, god of fire

6. Mars, god or war

7. Hypnos, god of sleep

8. Tantalus, who was plunged chin deep in water with fruit over his head just out of reach.

9. Hercules, hero of superhuman strength who performed 12 labours

10. Flora, goddess of flowers

Exercise 6.7

1. antiquarian
2. disciplinarian
3. nonagenarian
4. egalitarian
5. grammarian
6. librarian

Exercise 6.8

These are examples only:

1. My 69-year old grandpa isn't keen on becoming a septuagenarian.
2. Fruit bats, which are fruitarian, are common in Australia.
3. In Northern Ireland the distance between Protestant and Catholic is sometimes referred to as a sectarian divide.
4. Mr Creakle in *David Copperfield* was an authoritarian headmaster.
5. Because veterinarian is so hard to say most animal owners just refer to the 'vet.'
6. The agrarian revolution introduced many new farming tools and methods at the end of the eighteenth century.

Exercise 6.9

1. complex
2. compound
3. simple
4. compound
5. complex
6. simple
7. complex
8. compound

Exercise 6.10

These are examples only:

1. I cried because I felt ill.
2. My mother, who is usually even tempered, was furious.
3. We were eating ice cream which we had bought from a mobile seller.
4. Although he broke his leg last year, Max is running.
5. As we really want to know, let's ask Rina who usually has inside information.

Exercise 6.11

These are examples only:

1. I laughed and I cried.

2. My mother was furious but my father didn't mind.

3. We were eating ice cream while Joanna's mother was in the shop.

4. Max is running as Fergal is swimming.

5. Let's ask Rina and then we'll decide.

Answer to anagram star on page 73.

Note: There is an error in the version printed in the book (1st impression, subsequently corrected in the re-print). The letters round the edge should be: T, T, R, N, I, S, O, A, Y.

The whole word, after this alteration, is <u>Stationary</u>. Here are 30 others to start you off. Pupils will think of more:

airy, anti, arty, astir, intra, natty, rain, rainy, rant, ration, rattan, ratty, rayon, roan, roar, roast, rota, rotary, saint, soar, stain, star, start, station, stoat, taint, toast, train, tsar, yarn

Chapter 7

Exercise 7.1

1. (a) taken over from, replaced.
    (b) lecture, thoughts, oration, presentation.
    (c) strong, sturdy, reliable.
    (d) casualness, not being too concerned.

2. (a) scrutiny
    (b) affectation
    (c) traversed
    (d) ill-omened

3. Holmes stays cheerful while Watson becomes depressed. Holmes has a wide general knowledge, such as Italian violin making. He refuses to jump to conclusions and he makes some kind of silent discovery by looking closely at the outside of the house while Watson remains mystified.

4. ill-omened, minatory, vacant, melancholy, blank, dreary, bleared.

    Note: There is an error in the first two printed versions of the book. It should read 'Which seven adjectives in the first three sentences...'

5. Holmes 'prattles' about the relative merit of two 18th century violin makers as he is refusing to think about the 'matter in hand' in order to keep his mind clear.

6. There is a policeman guarding the property and a group of idle onlookers ('loafers') around him who want to find out what is going on, and so they are staring and listening.

Exercise 7.2

1. The architect Charles Barry redesigned the Westminster area.

2. It had a tidal river with extensive navigability which made it convenient for shipping.

3. They formed many guilds and livery companies relating to retail and other trades, such as weaving and candle making, many of which still exist.

4. At Crécy and Agincourt England fought against France and won.

5. England's major exports were wool and leather.

6. The Council misguidedly demolished many fine old buildings and replaced them with modern monstrosities. Earlier, German bombing had destroyed buildings too, but it is an ironic comparison because the GLC was not supposed to be an enemy 'attacking' London.

7. Romans occupied the present City of London and walled it. Later, when the Romans had gone, the Saxons disliked the City of London and so established their government at Westminster.

8. During the Tudor period Londoners experienced the Wars of Succession (they fought over who would be the next monarch) which wasted resources. Henry VIII destroyed the monasteries to get more money. There were shifts between Protestantism and Catholicism, each one involving much religious persecution. All this led to mass unemployment and poverty, which was followed by millions of deaths in plague epidemics.

Exercise 7.3

1. It is dawn, which you know because the poem talks of the 'beauty of morning'. It says that no one is up, it is 'silent' and houses 'seem asleep.' Further, work has not begun because the air is 'smokeless'. Finally, the poem begins to describe sunrise, as it mentions 'first splendour' and the 'mighty heart [of London] is still.'

2. Any four of: fair, touching, beauty, bright, glittering, beautifully, splendour, and calm (a case could be made for others too).

3. Wordsworth writes of the city wearing the beauty of the morning and having a heart (which suggests the life of the city); the sun soaking the fields and air (which suggests the sun is kindly); the river having a will of its own (which suggests that the river is not governable, although it can be used); and the houses sleeping (using houses as a metonym for occupants).

4. Wordsworth can see churches, palaces, theatres and law courts as he talks of 'towers, domes, theatres and temples'.

5. The phrase 'Open unto the fields…' suggests how much smaller London was in 1802.

Exercise 7.5

lasso (Spanish)
hippo (Abbreviation)
soprano (Italian)
embryo (Double vowel – y counts here)
kangaroo (Double vowel)
biro (Often assumed to be Spanish – actually Hungarian. Laszlo Biro, inventor of ball point pen – see page 10)
tattoo (Double vowel)
radio (Double vowel)
scenario (Italian)
albino (Spanish)

Exercise 7.6

These are examples only:

1. We have a navicular plant trough in our garden.
2. The British navy, often called The Senior Service, was founded in the seventeenth century.
3. Early navigators sailed the world and made maps.
4. There is a deep navigational channel in the centre of many large rivers.

1. Before the eruption of Pompeii in AD 76 many people were evacuated to safety.
2. Some people say my manner is abrupt, but actually I just try to be direct and truthful.
3. We managed, for once, to get to the end of the lesson without being interrupted by visitors.
4. Peace talks were proceeding well when suddenly there was a rupture.

Exercise 7.7

1. Namby pamby: insipid, weakly or sentimental. It was the nickname of Ambrose Phillips, 1674–1749, who wrote verse addressed to babies.

2. Hanky panky: suspicious behaviour (sometimes sexual). It is a corruption of hocus pocus. (See below.)

3. Wishy washy: lacking in force or substance, watery. The origin is unknown. (It could be fun to invite pupils to speculate.)

4. Willy nilly: of something that will be done whatever happens. Literally 'will he or will he not' from the Latin *volens nolens*.

5. Shilly shally: indecisive. It's a corruption of 'shall I, shan't I?'.

6. Niminy piminy: affectedly refined. Derived from *The Heiress* (1786) in which a character was told to keep saying it before a mirror as an elocution exercise.

7. Airy fairy: fanciful, unrealistic. From Tennyson's poem *Lillian* (1830).

8. Hocus pocus: something false. It is a magic word used by a conjuror; probably a parody of *Hoc est corpus meum* (this is my body) from the Latin mass. The word 'hoax' comes from it.

Exercise 7.8

1. The plans were completed by the architect before the end of the month.
2. The ball was hit a long way by the hockey player with her stick.
3. Some biscuits were made by Nathan.
4. London was taken by William of Normandy in 1066.
5. The old lady was knocked down by the motorcyclist.
6. The electronic whiteboard was cleared by Mrs Johnson.

Exercise 7.9

Mary Swavesey and her sisters erected the conservatory. Gail had measured and levelled the site. Emma had prepared the sections of the conservatory. Then the three sisters, working together, put the conservatory in place. Mr Newington had ordered it and paid for it. He praised them for a fine piece of work.

Exercise 7.10

These are examples with the objects underlined:

1. The Victorians supervised the <u>building of the London sewers</u>.
2. Omnibuses crossed <u>Tower Bridge</u>.
3. The Port of London enjoyed <u>prosperity</u>.
4. I asked <u>the Mayor of London</u>.
5. We represented <u>her family</u>.
6. My mother saw <u>the latest Harry Potter film</u>.

Exercise 7.11

This is an example only:

'Is that Tower Bridge?' asked Lee, who came from California and who had not been to London before.

'Yes, although a lot of tourists mistake it for London Bridge because it looks so dramatic,' replied Mike, gathering up his briefcase, mobile phone, papers and umbrella in preparation for getting off the train.

'Goodness! How exciting! I'll have a walk across it, maybe, and take some photographs after our meeting,' said Lee.

Chapter 8

1. About 600 people lived in the village of Maekung (100 families).

2. Her breast milk is drying up because there is not enough food. She doesn't want to admit it even to herself. (But pupils may come up with more ingenious ideas. The question invites speculation.)

3. Jinda misses laughter most from earlier years.

4. Ghan went to the city to get a job.

5. This is an example only: Rows of villagers, mostly women, are scything by hand wearing sarongs and hats. It is very hot. Their babies lie at the edge of the field in the shade. There is a happy atmosphere when the harvest is good.

6. In a good year, the villagers sell the surplus rice crop to buy items such as livestock, clothing, and modest luxuries, such as honey.

7. Minfong Ho describes Dao's wedding because of the contrast it provides. It was a happy, hopeful time compared with the anxieties of the present.

Exercise 8.2

1. The ship is sailing north, which you know because the south wind is blowing behind them and thus must be pushing them north, rather than them facing it as they sailed south.

2. The ship cannot proceed because there is no wind / breeze.

3. (a) hollo: a call like 'hello' or 'hey'
   (b) rose (verb)

4. Coleridge uses the two six-line verses to spin out the agony and drama. The emphasis is on the longer verses.

5. These are examples:

   'Silence of the sea'. The glassy, long vowels suggest stillness and the repeated 's' (sibilance) suggests menace.

   'Breeze to blow'. The repetition of 'b' is a lively (plosive) and jerky movement, like the ship which starts and stops.

6. The poem is in ballad form, which was the traditional form used for stories for centuries. Coleridge deliberately chooses a medieval form to tell a story about life, death, guilt, curses etc. The rhyme drives the narrative forward like the ship when it is moving and like the ancient mariner's agony when the ship is still.

Exercise 8.3

1. Kundal is in North West India.

2. Kundal last experienced heavy rainfall in 1998.

3. Each individual receives one fifth of a kilo of both maize and wheat.

4. The government 'drought relief work' programme has made things harder for the villagers because it involves time-wasting bureaucratic assessment of eligibility.

5. The government is building a dam and has opened ration shops.

6. (a) unable to read and write.
   (b) a long way from cities, towns and airports.

Exercise 8.5

These are examples only:

Sadly the drought recurred in three successive years.
We could see that the problem was recurring.

I inferred that she thought my answer was correct.
You are inferring from what I said that I agree with you, but I don't.

The hockey match had to be deferred because of bad weather.
We watched our teacher deferring to the headmistress's authority.

The road was barred so we had to find another route.
Barring hold-ups, I will be there at 7.00 pm.

We referred to the big dictionary in the library and found what we were looking for.
I think my aunt was referring to an earlier visit.

Exercise 8.6

These are examples only:

1. My baby sister fell while I was looking after her so I felt very culpable. (*culpo* I blame)
2. I got the impression that the teacher was hostile to our idea for a class end-of-term party. (*hostis* an enemy)
3. My brother fights less now but he is still too pugnacious for his own good. (*pugno* I fight)
4. It is puerile to argue about silly little things like an infant when you're 13 years old. (*puer* a child)
5. Fraternal twins are not identical. (*frater* a brother)
6. His caprine behaviour, as he frolicked in the field, made us all laugh. (*capra* a goat)
7. Henry V was a somewhat belligerent king, according to Shakespeare, who depicts him marching into France to war as if it's a perfectly reasonable thing to do. (*bellum* war)
8. People with sedentary jobs such as office work should make sure they get some exercise to make up for all that sitting. (*sedeo* I sit)
9. I knew it was a military town because I noticed the barracks as we drove past. (*miles* soldier)
10. I try to be veracious but it is sometimes difficult to tell the truth when it's going to hurt people's feelings. (*verax* truthful)

Exercise 8.7

Sighing, she bent (to work).
She bent to work, sighing.

Across the valley, yellow rice fields stretched, (stooped and dry).
Yellow rice fields, stooped and dry, stretched across the valley.

Before Astha's involvement, the illiterate and geographically remote people of Kundal did not know (their rights).
The illiterate and geographically remote people of India did not know their rights before Astha's involvement.

Day after day, day after day, we stuck, (nor breathe nor motion; as idle as a painted ship upon a painted ocean).
We stuck day after day, day after day (nor breathe nor motion; as idle as a painted ship upon a painted ocean).

There is nothing wrong with any of these sentences. The sentences simply have different emphases. The sentence opening tends to be more direct if started with the subject, but it is best to vary syntax and start with both the subject and object on occasion, as it is dull if a whole series of sentences are similarly shaped.

Exercise 8.8

These are examples only:

1. Together, Jinda and Dao walked home.
2. After the storm, shoots began to sprout from the wet ground.
3. For many years, my grandparents lived abroad.
4. Near our school, is a massive, old oak tree.
5. Armed with a broom, the woman drove the fox away from her hens.
6. Puzzled, I opened the parcel.
7. Beneath the flames, we could see the outline of an old box.
8. In the morning light, stood the postman, silhouetted in the porch.

Exercise 8.9

These are examples only:

1. Much-visited
2. well-thumbed
3. guidebook-clutching
4. American-made
5. fresh-drawn
6. lesson-weary (teachers)

Chapter 9

Exercise 9.1

1. Five people were present at this interview.

2. They were the narrator (David), Mr Creakle, Mrs Creakle, Miss Creakle and the man with the wooden leg.

3. Mr Creakle did not see David alone because he is a coward and a bully. After the reports of David from Mr Murdstone, he may have been worried that David might bite him too and so wanted others there to restrain David if necessary. He also wanted an 'audience' to see him demonstrating his power and he probably thought that it would be more menacing for David if he had to face several people.

4. Mrs Creakle and Miss Creakle are thin and quiet. David realises they are gentle, kindly and sympathetic when they're 'not disappointed' that he has done nothing wrong yet and he later sees them wiping their eyes in distress. He feels sorry for them, as well as them sympathising with him.

5. (a) brute, dragon, ogre etc.
   (b) reject, jettison etc.
   (c) hesitated, stammered etc.
   (d) hurriedly, hastily etc.

6. Everyone except Mr Creakle is being bullied. He has forced his own family to be present, he speaks to the man with the wooden leg only to snarl orders and bullies David in the most obvious manner.

7. These are examples only: The narrator is relieved, frightened, insecure and threatened.

Exercise 9.2

1. The narrator is a person who has met someone ('a traveller') who's been to Egypt.

2. The statue is a pair of huge stone pillars, once legs, on a plinth with a caption. The head, on which an authoritarian face is still visible, is broken off and lying separately nearby.

3. (a) torso-less, bodiless etc.
   (b) face, features etc.

4. Encourage pupils to range widely: they may comment on alliteration, the remoteness of the scene and the choice of word 'colossal', which might encourage a comparison with Colossus of Rhodes.

5. This poem has been included in a chapter focusing on bullying because Ozymandias was clearly a bully, or presented as such by the traveller and narrator. This is portrayed in the description of his visage with its 'wrinkled lip', its 'sneer of cold command' and the aggressive statement on the pedestal.

Exercise 9.3

1. (a) The purpose of this writing is to help / inform adults concerned about children being bullied.
    (b) It is suitable for this purpose because it is written in very clear English and is addressed directly to parents.

2. The writer has included bullet points to break up the information and to make the message clear and easy to read, as some parents will not be good readers and others will not be native English speakers.

3. Parents should set a good example, they should talk to their child, they should make careful notes and they should contact their child's school.

4. A child might bully others because he / she is troubled by events in his / her own life and is taking his / her feelings out on others. A child can be a bully because he / she does not know how to mix normally. A child can be a bully because he / she imitates the behaviour of others, for example, parents or other friends.

5. Example is important because bullying is learned behaviour and children copy parents and other adults. So it is important that they set the right example.

6. There is no pre-judgement here – see what the pupils suggest.

Exercise 9.5

These are examples only:

1. Sir Colin Davis stands on a podium when he conducts the London Symphony Orchestra.
2. All vertebrates are quadrupeds, although the four legs have almost disappeared in snakes.
3. Crayfish and lobsters are arthropods because they have jointed legs.
4. I have booked a pedicure because I want my feet to look good on holiday.
5. Digital pedometers are very fashionable just now because many people are keen to count the number of steps they take in a day.
6. There is a huge pediform sculpture at Penshurst Place in Kent.
7. My brother, always interested in para-medical professions, has decided to study podiatry at university.
8. We toured central Paris in a pedicab and what fun it was to see someone else doing all the pedalling as we sat back and enjoyed the sights.
9. Sadly a centipede doesn't really have a hundred legs but it certainly has a lot.
10. Professional photographers often use a tripod to support the camera.

Exercise 9.6

These are examples only:

1. … we learn more.
2. … he went out to play football.
3. … Anna hadn't brought her music.
4. … he felt he could relax.
5. … I am going to read *Little Dorrit*.
6. … inspired Shelley's sonnet.

Exercise 9.7

These are examples only. The finite verbs are underlined:

1. Because he <u>had threatened</u> Matthew, …

2. A man who <u>loved</u> words, …

3. After she <u>had taken</u> lessons, …

4. However hard you <u>try</u> to ignore it, …

5. Although I <u>dislike</u> some Romantic verse, …

6. Once we <u>had paid</u> the bill, …

Exercise 9.8

These are examples only:

1. Income tax has to be paid regularly.
   Flowery patterns have come in this year.

2. When a friend is upset most of us try to help.
   I must set up a new email address.

3. He hit the bollard so sharply that he was lucky not to overturn the car.
   If you can't sleep, it sometimes helps to turn over.

4. New born kittens are helpless.
   I can solve these maths problems with less help than I used to need.

5. Many professional orchestras and choirs do outreach work in schools, helping children with music.
   If I need water in the night, I have only to reach out to the bedside table.

6. The outlook for tomorrow's weather is sunshine and showers.
   'Look out! There's something coming,' shouted my mother from the passenger seat.

Exercise 9.9

These are examples only:

1. My school, which has only 50 pupils, is small because it serves a thinly populated area.

2. Dickens, who married and had a large family, wrote many novels which feature children and childhood.

3. Our headmistress, who was appointed last year, has introduced an anti-bullying policy that is thorough, fair and sensible.

4. Shelley, who was only 30, died in 1822, the year in which *The Sunday Times* started.

5. Eat healthily if you want to feel well and enjoy life.

6. Mr Creakle, who was a horrible man, bullied David Copperfiesld.

Chapter 10

Exercise 10.1

1.   It is evening, which you can tell because the extract says the '…sun had set' and there was 'failing light' (line 38).

2.   Bigwig deliberately went down slope towards the fox pretending to be tired / injured in an attempt to divert the fox.

3.   Hazel is a decisive leader and a quick thinker, who is capable of anger. He is trusted by the other rabbits.

4.   (a) 'had quickened its pace'
     (b) 'aghast'
     (c) 'crafty predatory look'

5.   Bigwig is a very strong rabbit, who is needed by the others. His impulsive 'bravery' is not necessary and only succeeds in endangering himself and subsequently the others. Further, Bigwig disobeyed Hazel's orders.

Exercise 10.2

1.   A female hedgehog is a 'good mother' because she builds safe nests underground, leads out her young carefully when they are old enough, keeps them together and teaches them survival skills.

2.   Three characteristics that distinguish baby hedgehogs from adults are that the babies are helpless, blind and have soft white spikes.

3.   The writer's job was made difficult because hedgehogs constantly foul their nest and it is difficult to keep up with their feeding demands.

4.   The writer understood that he was overfeeding the hedgehogs because they looked bloated.

5.   Pupils could choose almost anything. These are examples only: the use of the word 'nursery' because it suggests human qualities; the image of the little fat creatures so full of milk that they can hardly move.

Exercise 10.3

1.   The narrator is addressing the 'tyger' (eighteenth century spelling of 'tiger').

2.   By 'fearful symmetry', the poet means the stripes and balance of the animal's body, which is symmetrical and beautiful, but the tiger is also a fierce predator. The oxymoron stresses this tension between the two aspects.

3.   The lamb contrasts with the tiger. The lamb is a small, gentle herbivore associated with meekness in comparison with the large, fierce meat eater.

4.   (a) hope, yearn, rise etc.
     (b) muscles, fibres, tendons etc.
     (c) the stand on which a blacksmith hammers metal.

5.   The word 'dread' is repeated for emphasis. Further, dread is a firm sounding word with its two 'd' sounds and short vowel. Dread is the narrator's main emotion. Dread has had a slight shift in meaning since the 18th century and was closer in meaning to 'awe' previously.

6. This is a religious poem because it says 'immortal hand or eye', which is a rerference to God. The narrator marvels that God, or nature, can be so varied as to create both lamb and tiger. The narrator also assumes an overall creator, which is referring to the biblical story in Genesis.

Exercise 10.5

1. historical
2. miracle
3. bicycle
4. physical
5. principle
6. hysterical

Exercise 10.6

1. practise
2. prophesy
3. licence
4. practice
5. license
6. prophecy

Exercise 10.7

These are examples only:

1. Most teachers hope that their lessons will inspire pupils.
2. I must return my library book because it is about to expire.
3. Should it transpire that I was right all along, I shall try not to laugh.
4. Catesby and others decided to conspire with Guy Fawkes and the result was the gunpowder plot.

Exercise 10.8

These are examples only:

Eating is enjoyable. (gerund)
A caterpillar is really just an eating machine. (gerundive)

After school in the summer, my favourite activity is playing outside. (gerund)
There aren't many playing instruments in the piano museum. (gerundive)

My mother likes walking. (gerund)
We took a walking holiday in the Pennines last year. (gerundive)

It isn't easy to find time for shopping. (gerund)
Would you like a shopping trip to Bluewater? (gerundive)

The Queen has given up riding in public. (gerund)
My new riding boots are brown. (gerundive)

My falling off the ladder was most unfortunate. (gerund)
My father is worried about falling share prices. (gerundive)

Exercise 10.9

1. The sea lifted smooth blue muscles of wave, as it stirred in the dawn light and the foam of our wake spread gently behind us, like a white peacock's tail. Glinting with bubbles, the sky was pale and stained with yellow on the eastern horizon. Ahead lay a chocolate brown smudge of land, huddled in mist with a frill of foam at its base. This was Corfu and we strained our eyes to make out the exact shapes of the mountains to discover valleys, peaks, ravines and beaches but it remained a silhouette.

2. 'That's Polly Pig,' she said, pointing to the sow nuzzling the straw in its pen. 'She's mine. My Dad gave her to me.' I leaned over the pen.
    'Yes, I know. You're a lucky girl. She looks a fine pig to me.'
    'Oh she is! She is!' The little girl's eyes shone with pleasure. 'I feed her every day and she lets me stroke her. She's nice.'
    'I bet she is. She looks nice.'
    'Yes, and do you know something else?' Tess's voice grew serious and her voice took on a conspiratorial tone. 'She's going to have babies in March.'